# KEKE PALMER

By Amy Davidson

Gareth Stevens
Publishing

**Please visit our website, www.garethstevens.com. For a free color catalog of all our high-quality books, call toll free 1-800-542-2595 or fax 1-877-542-2596.**

Library of Congress Cataloging-in-Publication Data

Davidson, Amy, 1988-
 Keke Palmer / Amy Davidson.
     p. cm. — (Rising stars)
 Includes bibliographical references and index.
 ISBN 978-1-4339-7284-3 (pbk.)
 ISBN 978-1-4339-7285-0 (6-pack)
 ISBN 978-1-4339-7287-4 (library binding)
 1.  Palmer, Keke—Juvenile literature. 2.  Motion picture actors and actresses—United States—Biography—Juvenile literature. 3.  Singers—United States—Biography—Juvenile literature.  I. Title.
 PN2287.P2245D38 2012
 791.4302'8092—dc23
 [B]
                                    2012011873

First Edition

Published in 2013 by Gareth Stevens Publishing
111 East 14th Street, Suite 349
New York, NY 10003

Copyright © 2013 Gareth Stevens Publishing

Designer: Ben Gardner
Editor: Ryan Nagelhout

Photo credits: Cover and all backgrounds Shutterstock.com; cover, p. 1 Christopher Polk/Getty Images; p. 5 John Sciulli/WireImage/Getty Images; pp. 7, 11 Vince Bucci/Getty Images; p. 9 J. Vespa/WireImage/Getty Images; p. 13 Featureflash/Shutterstock.com; p. 15 Raymond Boyd/Getty Images; p. 17 Alberto E. Rodriguez/Getty Images; p. 19 Frazer Harrison/Getty Images; p. 21 Arnold Turner/WireImage/Getty Images; p. 23 Kevin Mazur/WireImage/Getty Images; p. 25 Larry Busacca/Getty Images; p. 27 Robyn Beck/AFP/Getty Images; p. 29 Jemal Countess/Getty Images.

Printed in the United States of America

CPSIA compliance information: Batch #CS12GS: For further information contact Gareth Stevens, New York, New York at 1-800-542-2595.

# Contents

# Meet Keke

Keke Palmer is a talented singer and actress.

Lauren "Keke" Palmer was born on
August 26, 1993. She grew up in
Harvey, Illinois. She now lives in
Los Angeles, California.

# Getting Started

Keke began acting in the movie

*Barbershop 2* in 2004. She played

Queen Latifah's niece. It was only her

second audition ever!

# Hollywood Buzz

Keke starred in the movie *Akeelah and the Bee* in 2006 at the age of 13. She even sang on the soundtrack!

Keke won the NAACP Image Award for *Akeelah and the Bee* in 2007. She also won three other awards for the movie.

# Making Music

Keke signed with Atlantic Records in 2005. Her album *So Uncool* came out in 2007.

In 2007, Keke starred in the movie

*Jump In!* on Disney Channel. She also

sang two songs on the soundtrack.

More than 8 million people watched

the movie!

Corbin Bleu

## Branching Out

In 2008, Keke was a quarterback in the movie *The Longshots*. The movie tells the true story of Jasmine Plummer, a girl who wanted to play football with the boys.

Ice Cube

19

Keke played Jasmine. She trained for weeks to learn how to throw a football. Even Jasmine was impressed with her acting!

Jasmine Plummer

# True Calling

In 2008, Keke played True Jackson
in *True Jackson, VP* on Nickelodeon.
More than 4 million people watched
the show's first episode.

23

*True Jackson, VP* made Keke one of the most famous child actors on TV. She helped write the show's theme song. She sang it, too!

# Finding Her Voice

Keke starred in *Joyful Noise* in 2012. In the movie, she sang with stars like Queen Latifah and Dolly Parton!

Keke continues to make music and movies. She is the voice of a character in *Ice Age: Continental Drift*. She is also the voice of Aisha in the animated series *Winx Club* on Nickelodeon.

# Timeline

**1993**     Keke is born on August 26.

**2004**     Keke acts in her first movie, *Barbershop 2*.

**2006**     Keke stars in *Akeelah and the Bee*.

**2007**     Keke's album *So Uncool* comes out.

**2008**     Keke plays Jasmine Plummer in the movie *The Longshots*.
           *True Jackson, VP* starts on Nickelodeon.

**2012**     Keke stars in *Joyful Noise*.

# For More Information

## Books

Brooks, Riley. *All Access: Keke Palmer*. New York, NY: Scholastic, 2009.

Mattern, Joanne. *Keke Palmer*. Hockessin, DE: Mitchell Lane Publishers, 2011.

## Websites

### Keke Palmer on Twitter

*twitter.com/KekePalmer*

Follow Keke for the latest updates and photos from her life in Los Angeles!

### The Official Site of Keke Palmer

*kekepalmer.com*

Keep up with Keke as she posts news, photos, tour information, and more.

**Publisher's note to educators and parents:** Our editors have carefully reviewed these websites to ensure that they are suitable for students. Many websites change frequently, however, and we cannot guarantee that a site's future contents will continue to meet our high standards of quality and educational value. Be advised that students should be closely supervised whenever they access the Internet.

# Glossary

**animated:** a kind of movie that looks like a cartoon

**audition:** a short test to try out for a part

**award:** a prize given for doing something well

**episode:** one part of a TV show's story

**soundtrack:** the music from a movie

**theme song:** a song that begins a TV show

# Index